CODING ACTIVITIES FOR
DEVELOPING
MUSIC
WITH SONIC PI

Cathleen Small

ROSEN
PUBLISHING

T0018362

Published in 2022 by The Rosen Publishing Group, Inc.
29 East 21st Street, New York, NY 10010

Library of Congress Cataloging-in-Publication Data

Names: Small, Cathleen, author.
Title: Coding activities for developing music with Sonic Pi / Cathleen
Small.
Description: First edition. | New York : Rosen Publishing, 2022. |
Series: Code creator | Audience: Grade 7–12 | Includes bibliographical
references and index.
Identifiers: LCCN 2019008456| ISBN 9781725341050 (library bound) |
ISBN 9781725341043 (pbk.)
Subjects: LCSH: Sonic Pi (Computer file)—Juvenile literature. | Software
synthesizers—Juvenile literature. | Ruby (Computer program language)—
Juvenile literature. | Object-oriented programming (Computer science)—
Juvenile literature.
Classification: LCC ML74.4.S6 S63 2022 | DDC 781.3/4—dc23
LC record available at https://lccn.loc.gov/2019008456

Manufactured in the United States of America

Some of the images in this book illustrate individuals who are models. The depictions
do not imply actual situations or events.

CPSIA Compliance Information: Batch #CSRYA22. For further information contact Rosen Publishing, New York, New York at 1-800-237-9932.

Find us on

Contents

Introduction

Developing music has been part of human culture for thousands of years. Music has been discovered all over the world, in every culture, pretty much as far back as society extends. There is even evidence of prehistoric music, which originated before its creators were even literate.

Nowadays, people can use modern technology, including computers, to mix and make music, but music itself has been around for as long as humankind.

As centuries and millennia have passed, music development has evolved. More instruments have been invented, knowledge of music theory has expanded, synthesizers have enabled musicians to create sounds electronically, and now technology has enabled composers to create music using nothing more than their computer. That is not to say that music is no longer composed the old-fashioned way, with musicians sitting around playing instruments and composing on the fly. It simply no longer *has* to be done that way. Amateur and professional composers can use software and applications to create music on their desktop computer, laptop, tablet, or even smartphone.

In the era of advanced music technology, a lot of work is done with software. For example, Pro Tools is a well-known digital audio software suite that can be used for recording and sound production. Sibelius is another example of a music composition software package. Logic Pro is a Mac-based professional recording studio that exists right on one's own computer. There are many, many other music production software packages and applications available today, some of which are available as web-based applications that can be accessed from any computer or similar device.

Music mixing and music creation software is available for every computing platform. To get really into the finer details of creating sound, aspiring musicians can code to create songs.

What about those interested in coding to develop music? What about people who want to couple their interest in computer science with their love of making music? While there are not as many applications that support this endeavor, they do exist. One interesting application like this is Sonic Pi, which was built in collaboration with teachers for use in the classroom and for those new to coding for music development.

Sonic Pi is free to use. The idea behind the software is that it uses music development to teach basic computing concepts. Not only does this allow users to combine musical creativity with some simple instruction on coding, but it also introduces aspiring coders to an easy-to-use language that will provide a solid foundation of knowledge if they go on to learn more complex coding languages.

Sonic Pi touts itself as being powerful enough for professional musicians, but simple enough for new coders to learn. The programming language

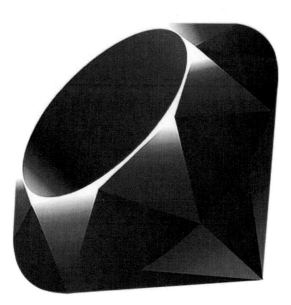

Ruby is a popular programming language that was developed in the 1990s. Sonic Pi is an integrated development environment that uses Ruby syntax to produce music.

used is Ruby, but Sonic Pi is the integrated development environment (IDE) that uses Ruby syntax to produce music. Ruby is an object-oriented programming language that was first developed in the 1990s.

Ruby is a highly popular programming language, and it often makes lists of top ten most popular coding languages. Learning Ruby in the context of developing music with Sonic Pi allows users to learn the fundamentals of a programming language that is widely used in the greater technology field.

The beauty of combining music and coding is that the feedback is both immediate and enjoyable. It does not take long to code a simple melody, repeating rhythm, or bass line, and users can quickly check their work by making sure the tune plays as intended. More than that: it is just plain fun to create music.

Downloading and setting up Sonic Pi is pretty simple. On the home page at https://sonic-pi.net, there are download links for Windows, Mac, and Raspberry Pi versions of the application. Simply click on the button for the appropriate version, and the site will begin the process of downloading and installation.

After downloading Sonic Pi and installing it in the correct directory, launch the application. At the top of the interface, there is a coding window with Run, Stop, Record, Save, and Load buttons at the top left. On the top right, there are six other useful option buttons, including the all-important Help button.

The Help button will toggle on and off the Help pane at the bottom of the screen. This pane is full of examples, synths, effects (commonly referred to as FX), and samples. There is also a useful tutorial for new users. The tutorial is basically like a user guide; click on any topic to reveal an explanation in the bottom-right pane.

If you get stuck at any point, visit the robust Sonic Pi community, where it is possible to find useful information and support from countless Sonic Pi users.

Activity 1

Creating a Live Loop

Sonic Pi is built around the idea of live loops. In most songs, especially in popular genres, there is a melody that is more or less repeated—or looped— numerous times throughout the course of the song. The same general beat exists throughout the song, although sometimes there are segments of a song that break up the established beat a bit. As a general rule, however, songs consist of looping melodies.

In Sonic Pi, the syntax (or language structure) for a live loop contains the name of the loop, the keywords "do" and "end" to mark where the live loop starts and where it ends, and then some syntax for the body of the loop, which basically explains what the loop will be repeating. Coded together, those four components look like this:

```
live_loop :MyBeat1 do
      sample :ambi_piano, rate: 1.5
      sleep 0.5
end
```

Copy this code into Sonic Pi and click Run to hear the loop. Clicking Stop will, as expected, stop the loop.

Note the indentation of the body syntax. After typing "do" on the first line and hitting the return key, Sonic Pi will automatically indent the next line appropriately. When typing "end" and pressing the return key, Sonic Pi will automatically outdent the code so it is again flush with the indentation at the start of the loop. Properly indented code is important for readability, and for many programming languages, it is also required for the program to run. Sonic Pi takes away the hard work and does much of the indenting and outdenting for its users.

On the first line of the code snippet above, ":MyBeat1" is the name of the loop. Loops can be named anything, as long as the name consists of letters or numbers; using other symbols will cause an error and the loop will not run.

Typing the "sample" keyword on the second line prompts Sonic Pi to open a list of samples to choose from. Any and all of these samples will work the same in a live loop. Similarly, the rate at which the sample is played can be configured in this example—type in any number and see what happens. It is also possible to change the numeric value after "sleep" in the third line. This value determines how long the program will wait before playing the next note. Think of it as the tempo: lower sleep values will produce notes played in increasingly more rapid succession, and higher sleep values will produce a loop with a much slower tempo.

The rate value determines how quickly the note itself is played. For example, on the ambi_piano sample, a rate of 1.5 produces a result that sounds like a piano note being played. But if that rate is increased to 100, the note is played so quickly that it just sounds like a tap.

Make this live loop a little more interesting by adding a second instrument. After the end of the first live loop code, type the following:

```
live_loop :MyBeat2 do
    sample :drum_cowbell, rate: 1.5
    sleep 0.5
end
```

Click Run; now there is a cowbell layered above the piano. There can never be too much cowbell. Another cool feature of Sonic Pi is the ability to keep a loop playing while tweaking and adding to it. While the loop is still running, type the following lines into the code:

```
live_loop :MyBeat3 do
        sample :elec_bong, rate: 1.5
        sleep 0.5
end
```

Click Run again, and there it is—an electric bong sound laid on top of everything else. Learning live loops is important because they form the core of most musical creation in Sonic Pi. Being comfortable with making loops is one of the best ways to get more advanced, so feel free to experiment early and often.

Activity 2

Let's Make a Beep ... or Five

That first activity was a brief introduction to what Sonic Pi can do, but to really get comfortable with the application, it is time to go back to the basics—starting with simple beeps. When learning to play an instrument, the first, most basic skill is the ability to play a note. For example, pressing one piano key one time is playing a note.

In Sonic Pi, synths are the name of the game. "Synth" is the short form of the word "synthesizer." In the context of making music, a synthesizer is something that creates sounds. Since digital audio workstations and other music-production applications have become popular, the number of synths at anyone's fingertips is almost limitless. Sonic Pi allows users to play around with many types of synths.

For this activity, start with a simple beep in Sonic Pi. This is the code to make that happen:

```
play 90
```

Actually, it is possible to substitute any number for "90." This would be equally acceptable:

play 75

Play around with the number a bit and one thing becomes obvious: the lower the number, the deeper the sound of the beep. Think of it like a piano, where the lower keys (on the left side of the keyboard) play low notes, and the keys at the high (right) end of the piano play high notes. The same is true with beeps in Sonic Pi.

Most music, though, does not consist of single notes. There might be pieces of a composition that consist of single notes played in succession, but most parts of any song consist of many different notes played together. If they are played simultaneously, it is considered a chord. When they are played in succession, the artist has created a melody.

Start here by playing a chord—a chord made of beeps. Sonic Pi makes this easy; just type several lines of beeps all at once, like this:

play 90
play 75
play 60

Click Run and there will be a beautiful chord. Well, maybe not all that beautiful, but a chord nonetheless. That is all there is to it. The numbers can be changed to create the chord that sounds best or fits into a composition's needs, so play around with this a bit before moving on to making a melody.

To create a melody, Sonic Pi needs to know not to play all the beeps at once. To give those instructions, add sleep intervals between the beeps. Sleeps tell Sonic Pi to wait for a designated period of time before playing the next note. For example:

```
play 90
sleep 1
play 75
sleep 1
play 60
```

This is a nice series of notes. However, it would probably be more interesting to create a melody of chords. Tweak the code above to tell Sonic Pi to play chords with sleep intervals between them to create a chord-based melody, like this:

```
play 90
play 80
play 70
sleep 1
play 75
play 65
play 55
sleep 1
play 60
play 50
play 40
```

That is definitely a bit more exciting. Want to speed it up? To do that, just change the sleep values. The rest between chords directly corresponds to the sleep number. A sleep value of "1" means Sonic Pi will rest for one second between notes or chords. A sleep value of "0.5" would tell Sonic Pi to rest for half a second between notes or chords. Play around with the sleep value until achieving the perfect melody.

One other trick: if users know the names of the specific notes they are looking for, they can be directly input in Sonic Pi; they just need a colon in front of them. For example, to play the note C:

play :C

To play a sharp note, type an "s" after the name of the note. For example:

play :Cs

To play a flat, type a "b" after the note name, such as:

play :Gb

To play a chord, such as the C major chord (which consists of the notes C, E, and G), type this:

play :C
play :E
play :G

Activity 3

Playing with Synth Options

Using synths does not have to mean just entering notes or chords or building melodies. Sonic Pi allows users to deeply customize their sounds using numerous synth options.

Sonic Pi calls these options opts. Opts allow users to modify the basic sounds they create. Two common opts for modifying sounds are amplitude and pan.

Amplitude refers to the loudness of a sound. High amplitudes are loud, and low amplitudes are quieter. In Sonic Pi, amplitude is designated with numbers, with 0 being the lowest value. An amplitude of 0 plays, well, nothing. No sound at all. An amplitude of 1 is considered a standard volume. It is possible to enter higher amplitudes, but they will return rather distorted sounds. That is to protect the listener's ears; Sonic Pi will compress sounds that have too loud of an amplitude so that listeners are not exposed to anything too loud. It makes the sound unpleasant and probably not what was intended. Generally, amplitudes between 0 and 1 are best, with amplitudes below 0.5 typically producing the best results.

When using an opt in Sonic Pi, put a comma after the play value and then add in the desired opt. Using the beeps from the previous activity and adding in an amplitude opt would result in something like this:

play 75, amp: 0.5

The "amp:" tag has to be added to every line that should be modified. So this:

play 75, amp: 0.5
sleep 1
play 70

would result in only the first note having a specified amplitude. The second note would go back to the default amplitude value of 1. To modify the amplitude of both notes, it is necessary to type:

play 75, amp: 0.5
sleep 1
play 70, amp: 0.5

Another fun opt to experiment with is panning. Panning describes where in the stereo field the listener hears a sound. When listening to a song on the radio, it is often mixed so the melody appears to be surrounding the listener—equal on both sides. Sometimes, certain parts of the song will come out of the left speaker and certain parts out of the right. This kind of effect was quite common in the 1960s to 1980s, but it is less common today.

Panning is not used as obviously as it used to be, but when used for subtle effect, it can still add a lot of depth and creativity to a composition. In Sonic Pi, panning is determined by number values. A value of –1 indicates that the sound is panned all the way to the left; a value of 0 indicates that the sound is in the center of the stereo field; a value of 1 indicates that the sound is panned all the way to the right.

Just like with amplitude, panning is coded by putting a comma after a play value and then adding the pan opt, like this:

```
play 75, pan: -1
```

That would play a beep purely out of the left speaker. To really hear the effect of a sound moving across the stereo field, type this and then click Run:

```
play 75, pan: -1
sleep 0.5
play 75, pan: 0
sleep 0.5
play 75, pan: 1
```

This will produce a beeping sound that appears to be running across the stereo field, from left to right.

Activity 4

Switching Synths

Beeps are fun and a good way to start experimenting with Sonic Pi, but there are many other synths that can be used, too. In the bottom pane of the Sonic Pi interface, there are six options: Tutorial, Examples, Synths, FX, Samples, and Lang. Click on Synths.

Check out all the fun synths to play with. There is the default beep, but there are also things like Dull Bell, Hollow, Piano, Saw, and Zawa (a name that gives exactly no clues as to what it will sound like). Changing synths to explore some of these others is done with a very simple command: "use_synth."

When typing a command like "use_synth" into the Sonic Pi interface—and then pressing the spacebar—a menu will appear from which a synth can be chosen. However, it is also possible to simply type the name of the desired synth. Typing leaves room for error, so sometimes it is easiest just to select a synth from the list. Either way, the line to change synth sounds looks like this:

use_synth :zawa

This line has told the program to switch the synth sound to Zawa (whatever that is), but now it needs some additional instructions. Add in some play commands and some sleep commands to get an idea of what the sound can do. Take this for an example:

```
use_synth :zawa
play 75
sleep 0.5
play 60
sleep 0.5
play 75
sleep 0.5
play 70
sleep 0.5
play 65
sleep 0.5
play 60
```

After listening to this, it is obvious that Zawa produces some sort of futuristic sound—interesting.

Also interesting is the ability to switch synths in the middle of the melody by inputting another "use_synth" command. The "use_synth" command applies to all of the play calls that follow it, up until there is another instruction to change the synth. So if users do not want to use Zawa forever, they can throw in a different synth, like this:

```
use_synth :zawa
play 75
sleep 0.5
play 60
sleep 0.5
use_synth :chipbass
play 75
sleep 0.5
play 70
sleep 0.5
play 65
sleep 0.5
play 60
```

Play around with the different synths, and it will be obvious that it is possible to create some really fun, dynamic, and exciting melodies.

Envelopes: Not Just for Mailing Letters

The sleep command controls the time between sounds—but what about the time during sounds? How long does a note or chord play for? The duration of a note or chord is controlled by using an envelope. The longer name for this is ADSR (attack, decay, sustain, release) amplitude envelope, but musicians generally just use the shorter version. As suggested by its longer name, the envelope can also control amplitude.

Envelopes are kind of complicated because describing the duration of sound itself is complicated. Every note starts with silence; it also ends with silence. Of course, there is the part in between where the note is not silent. The time it takes for a sound to shift from being a sound to being silent is called the release.

In Sonic Pi, it is possible to modify the release. The greater the number for the release value, the longer the sound holds. The release opt works just like the amplitude and panning opts, and the best way to understand it is to play with some values. Type this and then click Run:

```
use_synth :zawa
play 70
sleep 0.5
play 70, release: 0.5
sleep 0.5
play 70, release: 1
sleep 0.5
play 70, release: 2
sleep 0.5
play 70, release: 5
```

Notice how much longer that final note lasts than the earlier ones? That is because the release was extended. Additionally, the sound fades out as the note progresses—in other words, the amplitude decreases as the note fades out.

What about fading a note in? It is possible to do that as well—that is called the attack. By default, the attack for any note is 0, meaning it goes from complete silence to the full amplitude of the note immediately.

Attack works like release: it is an opt that is added after the play command. Add an attack to the final two notes in a melody. Make the attack the same length as the release, and then click Run. The code should look something like this:

```
use_synth :zawa
play 70
sleep 0.5
play 70, release: 0.5
sleep 0.5
play 70, release: 1
sleep 0.5
play 70, attack: 2, release: 2
sleep 0.5
play 70, attack: 5, release: 5
```

Notice that it is possible to have multiple opts for any play command. If a song called for it, Sonic Pi would allow there to be amplitude and panning opts at the same time as well—each one just needs to be separated by a comma.

Normally, when the attack and release opts are used, the note peaks at its highest amplitude in the middle. A diagram of the sound envelope would look like a triangle: if zero is the baseline, a line (designating the sound) would climb upward in the attack phase of the note. At the highest amplitude (the middle), it would reach a peak, and then it would start going back down to the baseline on release—thus making a triangle. However, what if the note should be held at the highest amplitude for a longer time, making the diagram look more like a trapezoid? This can be adjusted by using the sustain opt.

Add a sustain opt in with the other opts that have been modifying the notes. For simplicity's sake, use the same value for sustain as those for attack and release. The last three lines of code should now look like this:

```
play 70, attack: 2, sustain: 2, release: 2
sleep 0.5
play 70, attack: 5, sustain: 5, release: 5
```

Now click Run and listen to the notes. Pretty interesting stuff, huh?

Activity 6

Sampling with Sonic Pi

Sonic Pi gives users the power to create their own custom sounds, but it also lets them use and modify prerecorded sounds. These are called samples.

Samples are often used in popular music. The pop, electronic, and hip-hop genres are notorious for using samples from older, sometimes obscure songs to make backbeats or hooks.

Sonic Pi contains more than a hundred samples users can play with and incorporate into their music. Clicking on Samples in the menu at the bottom of the screen brings up a list of them.

Alternatively, it is possible to insert a sample by just typing "sample" in the Sonic Pi window and pressing the space bar. After, a menu will appear with all of the prerecorded samples to choose from. Pick whichever one looks interesting, and then click Run to see what it sounds like.

Just like with notes or chords, it is possible to layer multiple samples on top of each other. Type the following and then click Run:

```
sample :ambi_glass_rub
sample :bass_thick_c
sample :ambi_choir
```

This produces a creepy sound that might be right at home as background music for a scary movie, right?

Just as with synths, it is possible to add opts to samples to change their sound or duration. Do this to the samples we just layered on top of one another:

```
sample :ambi_glass_rub, amp: 0.5, pan: -1
sample :bass_thick_c, amp: 1, pan: 0
sample :ambi_choir, amp: 0.5, pan: 1
```

The difference here is subtle, so adjust the attack and release to make a more pronounced change. Alter the code to look like this:

```
sample :ambi_glass_rub, amp: 0.5, pan: -1, attack: 3, release: 3
sample :bass_thick_c, amp: 1, pan: 0, attack: 6, release: 6
sample :ambi_choir, amp: 0.5, pan: 1, attack: 3, release: 3
```

Now the tension is starting to build in the sound. It is getting creepier.

It is also possible to speed up or slow down samples in Sonic Pi. The rate opt adjusts the speed. A rate of 1 is standard; anything less than 1 slows down the sample, and anything greater speeds it up.

Since good creepy music builds slowly, it will be best to slow down the samples. Add a rate opt of 0.5 to each sample, like this:

```
sample :ambi_glass_rub, amp: 0.5, pan: -1, attack: 3, release: 3,
    rate: 0.5
sample :bass_thick_c, amp: 1, pan: 0, attack: 6, release: 6, rate: 0.5
sample :ambi_choir, amp: 0.5, pan: 1, attack: 3, release: 3, rate: 0.5
```

Now things are really getting scary. Maybe this sampling could be used as the score for a horror movie—and maybe it should speed up as the villain draws closer to the victim. It is possible to repeat the sample but change the rate.

Sonic Pi gives users the ability to copy and paste lines, so rather than retyping the example, just copy those three lines and paste them two more times, which makes a total of nine lines. Make sure the rate on the first three lines is set at 0.5, the second three lines is set at 1.5, and the final three lines is set at 2.5. Then go back and insert a sleep line between each group of three. Set it at 0.05 because the break between sample groups should be very short. The code now looks like this:

```
sample :ambi_glass_rub, amp: 0.5, pan: -1, attack: 3, release: 3,
    rate: 0.5
sample :bass_thick_c, amp: 1, pan: 0, attack: 6, release: 6, rate:
    0.5
sample :ambi_choir, amp: 0.5, pan: 1, attack: 3, release: 3, rate: 0.5
sleep 0.05
sample :ambi_glass_rub, amp: 0.5, pan: -1, attack: 3, release: 3,
    rate: 1.5
sample :bass_thick_c, amp: 1, pan: 0, attack: 6, release: 6, rate: 1.5
sample :ambi_choir, amp: 0.5, pan: 1, attack: 3, release: 3, rate: 1.5
sleep 0.05
sample :ambi_glass_rub, amp: 0.5, pan: -1, attack: 3, release: 3,
    rate: 2.5
sample :bass_thick_c, amp: 1, pan: 0, attack: 6, release: 6, rate: 2.5
sample :ambi_choir, amp: 0.5, pan: 1, attack: 3, release: 3, rate: 2.5
```

It may sound a little choppy, so play with values to smooth it out. Notice anything else a little weird? The final set of samples sounds a bit lower than the first two sets. That is because of the rate. When the rate is adjusted, it will sometimes change the octave of the sample—just something to keep in mind.

Activity 7

Randomizing Music

Another fun way to customize music in Sonic Pi is to randomize it. The melody in most songs is typically fairly predictable but does not often stay exactly the same the whole time. There are random—but predictable—elements in it.

Sonic Pi allows users to do the same in their compositions. It has a randomization feature, though it is not truly random—it repeats in a somewhat expected pattern. (Truly randomized music is not exactly pleasant to the ear—humans like some predictability in their music.)

Since it was so much fun to play with creepy sounds in the previous activity, that theme will carry over here. Live loops will also make their return. Type out the following code and click Run:

```
loop do
      sample :ambi_haunted_hum, rate: (rrand 0.125, 3)
      sleep rrand(0.2, 2)
end
```

Creepy, right? As may be obvious, the rrand command is what tells Sonic Pi to randomize the sound. The two numbers after it are the minimum and maximum values. In the second line, rrand is applied to the rate, and Sonic Pi is instructed to randomize the rate of the sample between the values of 0.125 (slowest) and 3 (fastest). In the third line, Sonic Pi is instructed to randomize the rate of sleep between the least amount of time (0.2) and the most (2). Sonic Pi will never randomize outside of these two parameters in each instance—the rate, for example, will never go below 0.125 or above 3.

Another way to use randomization is to choose from a list of items. For example, suppose a composition needs to randomize between a few different samples. The choose command can be used and passed to a list of samples, from which it will choose one. The code would look like this:

```
loop do
      sample choose([:ambi_haunted_hum, :ambi_choir,
       :vinyl_backspin, :glitch_robot1])
      sleep rrand(0.2, 2)
end
```

Click Run and listen to what this produces. Sure, it is a little weird, but everyone has different tastes!

Activity 8

A Little Advanced Programming

Sonic Pi is built on the Ruby language. Ruby is very flexible, which means there is a lot that can be done with it after mastering its basic syntax and structures.

One such structure is the code block. A block is just a chunk of several (or more) lines of code. Why might someone want to group code into blocks? Well, doing so makes it easy to make changes to a larger group of lines, rather than one at a time. Many things in Sonic Pi, such as amplitude, revert to a certain default value if modifications are not applied on each line. With a code block, however, it is possible to make an attribute apply to every line in the block.

Code blocks are set off with "do" and "end" commands. For example:

```
do
        sample :ambi_dark_woosh
        sleep 0.5
        play 75
        sleep 0.5
        sample :ambi_lunar_land
end
```

Click Run with just this code block, and nothing happens. That is because Sonic Pi does not yet know what to do with this particular block. However, setting up the block is all that is necessary for now—it can be used later.

One useful modification to make to a code block is to make it repeat a certain number of times. To repeat, just add code in front of the do. Repeat this code block five times by adding "5.times" to the first line, so the code looks like this:

```
5.times do
      sample :ambi_dark_woosh
      sleep 0.5
      play 75
      sleep 0.5
      sample :ambi_lunar_land
end
```

Now when Run is clicked, the code block executes five times. It is also possible to just execute a code block an infinite number of times. Instead of typing something like "5.times" or "10.times," just type "loop," so the first line would look like:

```
loop do
```

Using a plain loop command, however, means the loop will never exit, and anything that is typed after the end command will not execute.

Moving back to the loop that executed five times: after the end statement, add a line calling a different sample, like this:

```
5.times do
        sample :ambi_dark_woosh
        sleep 0.5
        play 75
        sleep 0.5
        sample :ambi_lunar_land
end
sample :ambi_swoosh
```

Pretty neat, right? The loop executes five times, and then the composition finishes up with an ambi_ swoosh sound effect.

Another fun thing to do is to use conditionals. In programming, there is a structure often called if-then, in which the coder essentially tells the computer: if something specific happens, then do this. For example: if the user enters "yes" to Question 5, then ask them to complete a survey.

Sonic Pi allows users to do the same type of thing with music. In music, though, it is not likely that the listener will be asked a question. What might be done, however, is wrapping a conditional in with a randomization. For example, you might want Sonic Pi to essentially flip a coin and decide to play one sample or another randomly. There is a function called one_in that allows users to specify probability. The code one_in(2) basically means a probability of 1 in 2, or 50 percent; one_in(4) basically means 1 in 4, or 25 percent, and so on.

Suppose a piece of music wants to randomly sample a piano and a cowbell, but the cowbell should show up more often. The loop for that could be written like this:

```
loop do
      if one_in(4)
            sample :ambi_piano
      else
            sample :drum_cowbell
      end
      sleep 1
end
```

Click Run and see how it sounds. Lots of cowbell and not so much piano, right? That is because the code essentially told Sonic Pi that, randomly, one in every four beats should be a piano, and when the beat was not a piano, it should be a cowbell. That leaves about three beats out of each four as a cowbell, and one as a piano note. Of course, this code is not telling the program which specific beats should have piano and which should have cowbell—i.e., every third beat should be piano—which is where the randomness comes in.

Activity 9

Let's Get into FX

One fun way to spice up a composition is to add effects, which in the music world are typically referred to as FX. (Get it? Same pronunciation, but a clever little abbreviation.)

Just as with samples and synths, Sonic Pi offers a robust library of premade FX. There is an FX tab at the bottom of the screen that displays them all. By double-clicking on one of the FX in the list, the bottom-right pane of the screen gives a description of the effect and shows how to code it in. Scrolling down in that pane will also display the opts that can be used to modify the effect.

Code blocks will come in handy here because FX are best applied to an entire block of code. Start by looking at echo, since that is an effect that is really easy to hear in a composition. Test it out with several samples and a beep, like this:

```
with_fx :echo do
        sample :drum_bass_hard
        sleep 0.5
        sample :elec_bong
        sleep 0.5
        sample :elect_plip
        sleep 0.5
        play 75
end
```

To really get a feel for the FX, play the same sounds right after, but without the echo. The code should now look like the following; this will play a nonecho version loop twice, just so the difference is noticeable:

```
with_fx :echo do
        sample :drum_bass_hard
        sleep 0.5
        sample :elec_bong
        sleep 0.5
        sample :elect_plip
        sleep 0.5
        play 75
end
2.times do
        sample :drum_bass_hard
        sleep 0.5
        sample :elec_bong
        sleep 0.5
        sample :elect_plip
        sleep 0.5
        play 75
end
```

A little echo makes a big difference. It is also possible to chain effects, which layers them on top of one another. All it takes is nesting one loop within another. Suppose a song needs a code block to have both a wobble and an echo effect; the code would look like this:

```
with_fx: wobble do
    with_fx :echo do
            sample :drum_bass_hard
            sleep 0.5
            sample :elec_bong
            sleep 0.5
            sample :elect_plip
            sleep 0.5
            play 75
    end
end
```

Note that each "do" command needs its own end statement. In this case, the first two lines both have "do" in them. That means the loop needs to end with two end statements, as it does here.

Another thing to remember is that FX can be altered by applying different opts. For example, maybe the echo effect should fade away slowly—that just requires adding in a decay time of ten beats to the line with the echo effect. Maybe the wobble effect needs to wobble faster. This can be accomplished by adjusting the wobble line's phase. Check out this updated code with FX opts:

```
with_fx: wobble, phase: 0.5 do
    with_fx :echo, decay: 10 do
            ample :drum_bass_hard
            sleep 0.5
            sample :elec_bong
            sleep 0.5
            sample :elect_plip
            sleep 0.5
            play 75
    end
end
```

Chords and Scales: Sonic Pi and a Little Music Theory

The first nine activities cover a lot about coding music in Sonic Pi, but to take music to the next level, the program also supports the use of chords, arpeggios, and scales. Now that is truly fancy.

Suppose, for example, the B minor chord was a core component of a composition. In Sonic Pi, simply type the following and click Run:

play chord(:B3, :minor)

This is not the most exciting sound ever, but it is a chord, and it can be modified by changing ":minor" to a variety of other values, such as ":dom7," which refers to the dominant seventh chord.

If that does not make much sense, do not worry. Sonic Pi does not require that users have a background in music theory to be able to play around with chords or recognize how different values affect the sound of the chord. That said, learning more about music theory would certainly be helpful for coding music in the program.

Sometimes, chords are played as arpeggios, which can also be utilized in Sonic Pi. Arpeggios use the "play_pattern" function. Type the following code into Sonic Pi and click Run:

```
play_pattern chord(:B3, :dom7)
```

The notes of the chord are now played in succession—making an arpeggio. This produces a very slow arpeggio, though. That is because the default separation between each note is a full second. The time between each note can be decreased, though, by using the function "play_pattern_timed" and a value less than 1. Type the following code—which includes both the original and the sped-up version, to show the difference—and click Run:

```
play_pattern chord(:B3, :dom7)
sleep 1
play_pattern_timed chord(:B3, :dom7), 0.1
```

There is quite a difference between the speeds. As the code's number values suggest, the separation between each note is 0.1 second instead of a full second.

Sonic Pi also allows users to play scales, which are another important part of music theory. Take the C major scale, for example, which is one of the most common in music. The C major scale is a good one to start with because all of the notes are natural, meaning there are no sharps or flats. (For those without a background in music theory, sharps and flats are made by the black keys on a piano. Natural notes are made with the white keys. So all of the notes in the C major scale are made using the white keys.)

The "play_pattern" function is used to play a scale, just as it is to play an arpeggio. Type the following into Sonic Pi and click Run:

```
play_pattern scale(:C3, :major)
```

The notes should gradually increase in pitch because C major plays, by default, as an ascending scale. Scales can also be played descending, which has its own set of advantages for making music.

In the meantime, this scale ascends pretty slowly. Again, just as with arpeggios, this can be changed by using the "play_pattern_timed" function. Change the code to look like this and then click Run:

```
play_pattern_timed scale(:C3, :major), 0.25
```

That speed is much better. The default separation between notes went from one second to 0.25 second, and now it sounds more like a real scale.

Another important component of Sonic Pi—and music theory in general—is the concept of octaves. Think of a piano, which has eighty-eight keys. The scale of C starts on a C note and steps up through C, D, E, F, G, A, and B. Seems simple enough—but there are several C notes on a piano. In fact, there are eight. The particular C that opens the scale determines the octave. If the scale begins with the C as far to the left of the keyboard as possible, it is starting at a low octave. Moving to the right across the keyboard to the next C, and then the next, and the next, increases the octave.

Sonic Pi, of course, supports multiple octaves. Want to hear C major go through all eight octaves? Alter the code to look like this and click Run:

```
play_pattern_timed scale(:C3, :major, :num_octaves: 8), 0.25
```

As a final exercise, it is time to combine the skills of creating a loop, adding a new synth that sounds like guitar notes being plucked, incorporating the C major scale, and using opts to modify the release value and some random cutoff and pan values. Type the following code into Sonic Pi and then click Run:

```
use_synth :pluck
loop do
        play choose(scale(:C3, :major)), release: 0.7, cutoff:
          rrand(60, 120), pan: rrand(-1,1)
        sleep 0.3
end
```

Play around with the values and different opts, and see how it affects the sound being produced. This particular one sounds a bit like something designed to soothe and calm.

Play around a lot with Sonic Pi—that is what it is designed for. It is possible to spend hours exploring the different functions and features and creating melodies, so have at it!

Career Connections

Sonic Pi is a whole lot of fun. Even those with little or no background in music theory or who do not play a musical instrument can quickly become composers using Sonic Pi. The prerecorded samples and preloaded synths and FX provide endless fodder for music creation. It is possible to create creepy effects, lilting melodies, thumping electronica, solid beats, and more.

The Ruby syntax used in Sonic Pi is not very difficult to learn and master. In the space of a few hours, it is easy to become fairly proficient at coding and creating in Sonic Pi. This is a real plus for a number of reasons. First, it means users can start creating music quickly. There is no great learning curve when it comes to using Sonic Pi. The tutorial in the app and the user forums are great places to go for questions and answers. Second, it means the activities here have provided a solid start at learning a very versatile programming language: Ruby. The language was developed in the early 1990s and is still very much used today. Part of the reason it has stuck around is because of its simplicity. Ruby was designed to be enjoyable to work with and to minimize confusion. Coding can be a very complex process, but Ruby was designed in large part to minimize complexity where possible. It was designed to be an intuitive tool for programmers—meaning one that does not frustrate its users.

In addition to being simple to learn, Ruby is also very robust. It runs on most operating systems, including all the major ones, such as Linux, macOS, Android, and Windows. It has all the features of a good general-purpose programming language, and it is capable of doing virtually anything any other general-purpose programming language can.

Ruby has quite a few alternate implementations as well as a popular web-application framework called Ruby on Rails. Many well-known websites

Ruby can run on Android, Linux, Mac, and Windows operating systems. These are by far the most widespread platforms to distribute any kind of program.

were built with Ruby on Rails. A few examples are: Airbnb, Shopify, Goodreads, Groupon, Hulu, Kickstarter, and, in its early days, even Twitter. In other words, coders who know Ruby have a very good chance at finding a job in the field of web development, should they choose to pursue it.

Ruby also happens to be very similar to Python, another widely used programming language, as well as Perl. Coders who master Ruby can fairly easily make the switch to Python or Perl and master those languages as well. When it comes time to look for a job, the more commonly used programming languages one is familiar with or proficient in, the better. The nice thing about programming languages is that after mastering one or two, it is relatively easy to transfer those skills to another language. Some of the basic principles remain the same across languages, even though the syntax differs.

There are a lot of things to do with knowledge of the Ruby coding language. If one enjoys the music end of things, there are numerous career opportunities available. The music industry itself has a number of different career paths for those interested in music technology, including audio technicians, sound designers, sound mixers, and digital audio editors. Some of these positions extend beyond the music industry, too. For example, sound designers work in music, but they also work in the entertainment and gaming industries since they are skilled at creating audio effects. Video games, for example, have both atmospheric effects, such as, perhaps, the typical background noises one would hear in a city for a game set in the heart of a city; and spot effects, such as explosions or footsteps.

One relatively new field for sound designers, who are also sometimes called sound editors or special effects editors, is virtual reality (VR). Virtual reality creates a simulation of an environment that must be extremely realistic so that users are fully immersed in the virtual world. For example, virtual travel is an interesting new piece of the industry—schools are using virtual travel to help children take virtual field trips to locations they cannot visit for real. For the experience to be useful, the virtual environment has to be as realistic as possible, which means the audio effects have to be spot on. A bird sound produced by a parakeet in an environment where that bird does not live, for example, would break the immersion and the entire experience would be weakened by improper effects.

The beauty of learning Ruby through Sonic Pi, though, is that music is far from the only career

Virtual reality (VR) is one of the newest and most exciting fields for coders to work in. There is even room for those interested in music to program for VR devices.

path available. Maybe music is a fun hobby, but you would prefer that your actual career be in some other field of coding. That is entirely possible, given how flexible Ruby is.

Nearly every industry has a need for coders because nearly every industry has some sort of technological presence or need. Someone interested in the field of medicine but not interested in being a doctor or nurse might decide to go into software development for the medical field. Virtual and augmented reality (AR) are becoming much more widely used in the medical field, and there is a great need for coders who can help develop VR and AR applications to train doctors or to help treat patients with particular phobias or other conditions. Similarly, AR solutions are being used to help guide surgeries, and numerous companies are hiring coders to help develop these programs. Or, if VR and AR are not an area of interest, there are other related coding opportunities in the health care field, such as building apps to track patient records or manage billing.

Maybe technology itself is an area of interest. There are countless opportunities in this industry as well. Major companies like Google, Microsoft, and Apple are always hiring coders in numerous departments, and a solid background in a general-purpose programming language will help anyone become a viable candidate.

In addition to major players, there are also smaller startup companies. Tech startups are a dime a dozen, and some will fail—but others will become giants in the industry. It is hard to tell which will fizzle and which will thrive, but either way, a solid background in programming will give any coder a chance to succeed.

Where is the best place to begin? Practicing these exercises with Sonic Pi was the start of a long path in programming. The best way to proceed now is to continue learning more about Ruby. With a greater mastery of this language, it is possible to branch out and learn other languages.

Down the line, it is important to do research and figure out if college is the correct choice for advancing your coding career. Although college is not a requirement for every coding job, it is definitely a big plus. Many, many more coding doors are open for those who obtain at least a bachelor's degree in computer science or a related field. There are many such programs out there, and not every one will break the bank. To be sure, there are some extremely expensive college programs out there— but they do not all cost a fortune, and scholarships and grants can help.

If music tech is your passion and your desire for your future job, there are even specialized courses and programs for that. For example, Berklee College of Music has several accredited degree programs that incorporate music technology. DigiPen Institute of Technology has an accredited computer science and digital audio degree program. The University of Illinois Urbana-Champaign has an accredited computer science and music degree. Note the emphasis on accredited here: any higher-education program should be hosted or sponsored by an accredited institution.

This is all a lot to think about. For now, take a deep breath and go back to Sonic Pi, learn more about Ruby, and have fun with the incredible technology that is available at your fingertips.

Glossary

arpeggio The notes of a chord played separately and in succession.

attack The initial portion of the sound in an ADSR envelope.

augmented reality A technology that overlays a computer-generated image on top of a user's view of the actual world.

chord Three or more notes played together.

composition A work of music, literature, or art.

digital audio workstation A device or application used to record, edit, and produce audio files.

integrated development environment A software application that allows programmers to develop other software; abbreviated IDE.

interface A program that allows users to communicate with a computer.

melody A specifically arranged sequence of notes, as in a song.

object-oriented Describing a type of programming language that uses objects as its basis.

octave A specific series of consecutive eight notes at different pitches.

operating system Software that supports a computer's basic functioning.

release The rate at which a synthesized sound drops to silence after the note is played.

samples Reused pieces of other songs within a composition.

scale An arrangement of notes in order by pitch.

sustain The volume of a produced note during the time period following the decay in an ADSR envelope.

syntax The arrangement of terms, functions, commands, variables, etc., that make up a programming language.

synthesizer An electronic musical instrument that can produce many different sounds.

virtual reality A computer simulation of an environment that users can interact with in a seemingly real way.

web-application framework A software framework that allows users to develop web applications and services.

For More Information

Canada Learning Code
129 Spadina Avenue
Toronto, ON M5V 2L3
Canada
Website: http://www.canadalearningcode.ca
Facebook: @CanadaLearningCode
Instagram and Twitter: @learningcode
Canada Learning Code is an organization that helps
    bring Canadians together with computer science
    and coding skills, hoping to encourage many to
    pursue careers in the technology industry.

CanCode
C. D. Howe Building
235 Queen Street, 1st Floor, West Tower
Ottawa, ON K1A 0H5
Canada
(800) 328-6189
Website: https://www.ic.gc.ca/eic/site/121.nsf
    /eng/home
Created by the government of Canada, CanCode is an
    organization that helps spread computer literacy
    across the country.

Codecademy
575 Broadway, 5th floor

New York, NY 10012
Website: http://www.codecademy.com
Facebook and Twitter: @Codecademy
Codecademy is an extremely popular online
    educational organization that features classes and
    tutorials and other educational opportunities for
    coders of all experience levels.

CreativeLive
228 Dexter Avenue North
Seattle, WA 98109
Website: https://www.creativelive.com
Facebook, Instagram, and Twitter: @CreativeLive
CreativeLive is an online community that offers
    many kinds of artistic classes for a fee. Its website
    features audio and music production classes.

Digital Media Academy
105 Cooper Court
Los Gatos, CA 95032
(866) 656-3342
Website: http://www.digitalmediaacademy.org
Facebook: @digitalmediaacademy.org
Instagram: @digitalmediaacademy
Twitter: @DMA_org
Digital Media Academy hosts camps all across the
    United States and Canada that teach young people
    how to code, the importance of computer science,
    and how technology will be used in the future.

Girls Who Code
28 West 23rd Street, 4th Floor
New York, NY 10010
Website: http://www.girlswhocode.com
Facebook, Instagram, and Twitter: @GirlsWhoCode
Despite a growing push, women are still widely
    underrepresented in the computer science
    industry. This organization helps connect girls and
    women to fields of technology and encourages
    them to pursue careers in coding.

Ruby on Rails
Website: https://rubyonrails.org
Twitter: @rails
Ruby—the language behind Sonic Pi—has been
    adapted into many different forms, and perhaps
    the most famous is Ruby on Rails. This web-
    development software suite is widely used and
    easy to learn.

For Further Reading

Anniss, Matthew. *The Impact of Technology in Music.* Portsmouth, NH: Heinemann, 2015.

Benedict, Aaron, and David Gallaher. *Using Computer Science in High-Tech Health and Wellness Careers.* New York, NY: Rosen Publishing, 2017.

Culp, Jennifer. *Using Computer Science in Digital Music Careers.* New York, NY: Rosen Publishing, 2018.

Dittmar, Tim. *Audio Engineering 101.* 2nd ed. New York, NY: Routledge, 2017.

Glendening, Isaac W., and Mary Glendening. *Makerspace Sound and Music Projects for All Ages.* New York, NY: McGraw-Hill Education, 2018.

Gonzales, Andrea, and Sophie Houser. *Girl Code: Gaming, Going Viral, and Getting It Done.* New York, NY: Harper Collins, 2017.

Hand, Carol. *Using Computer Science in High-Tech Criminal Justice Careers.* New York, NY: Rosen Publishing, 2017.

Kerr, Joanna, and DJ Booma. *How to Be a DJ in 10 Easy Lessons.* Lake Forest, CA: Walter Foster Jr., 2017.

Kolb, Tom. *Music Theory.* Milwaukee, WI: Hal Leonard, 2017.

Marji, Majed. *Learn to Program with Scratch: A Visual Introduction to Programming with Games, Art,*

Science, and Math. San Francisco, CA: No Starch Press, 2014.

Mooney, Carla. *Cool Careers Without College for People Who Love Music*. New York, NY: Rosen Classroom, 2014.

Moritz, Jeremy. *Code for Teens: The Awesome Beginner's Guide to Programming.* Herndon, VA: Mascot Books, 2018.

Niver, Heather Moore. *Careers for Tech Girls in Computer Science*. New York, NY: Rosen Publishing, 2015.

Whittemore, Jo. *Lights, Music, Code!* New York, NY: Penguin Workshop, 2018.

Bibliography

Aaron, Sam. "Sonic Pi: Live Coding Education." *The MagPi: Educator's Edition*. Retrieved February 16, 2019. https://sonic-pi.net/files/articles/Live-Coding-Education.pdf.

Aaron, Sam, and Carrie Anne Philbin. "Sonic Pi: API Cheatsheet v1.0." University of Cambridge Department of Computer Science and Technology. Retrieved February 16, 2019. https://www.cl.cam.ac.uk/projects/raspberrypi/sonicpi/media/sonic-pi-cheatsheet.pdf.

Gruendel, Hans. *Learn to Program with Sonic Pi: Edutainment Factory*. Amazon Digital Services, 2016.

Gruendel, Hans. *Making Music with Sonic Pi: An Edutainment Factory Book.* Amazon Digital Services, 2016.

Raspberry Pi Foundation. "Getting Started with Sonic Pi." Raspberry Pi Foundation. Retrieved February 16, 2019. https://projects.raspberrypi.org/en/projects/getting-started-with-sonic-pi.

Index

About the Author

Cathleen Small is the author of numerous nonfiction books for children and teens. Before turning to writing, Small was an editor of software, programming, and music technology books for a technical publisher. When she is not writing, Small enjoys traveling with her husband and two sons, as well as hanging out with her trusty pug and four mischievous cats.

Photo Credits

Cover ESB Professional/Shutterstock.com; cover, p. 1 (code) © iStockphoto.com/scanrail; p. 4 Yulia Grigoryeva/Shutterstock.com; p. 6 PrinceOfLove/ Shutterstock.com; p. 7 Yukihiro Matsumoto/The Ruby Logo/Ruby Community/CC BY-SA 2.5; p. 47 Rose Carson/Shutterstock.com; p. 50 © iStockphoto.com/MaximFesenko; interior pages border design © iStockphoto.com/Akrain.

Design: Matt Cauli; Editor: Siyavush Saidian; Photo researcher: Sherri Jackson